IMAGES
of America

McDUFFIE COUNTY

ON THE COVER: Local citizens gather around a float carrying Miss Thomson before a parade in Thomson. The man holding the Miss Thomson flag is Peter Knox, the young girl to his left is his daughter Hattie Emily Knox, and the man at far right is J.E. "Jim" Harrison Sr. (Courtesy of Edith Harrison Roth.)

IMAGES
of America

McDUFFIE COUNTY

Chase Norman Beggs

ARCADIA
PUBLISHING

ISBN 978-1-4671-0566-8

Published by Arcadia Publishing
Charleston, South Carolina

Printed in the United States of America

Library of Congress Control Number: 2020934633

For all general information, please contact Arcadia Publishing:
Telephone 843-853-2070
Fax 843-853-0044
E-mail sales@arcadiapublishing.com
For customer service and orders:
Toll-Free 1-888-313-2665

Visit us on the Internet at www.arcadiapublishing.com

This is dedicated to my wife, Nicole Jones Beggs; my son Bennett Blanchard Beggs; and those who inspired the book, both past and present.

Contents

ACKNOWLEDGMENTS

In an effort to preserve and archive the many images that tell the history of McDuffie County, I undertook the task of publishing this pictorial history of our past. This would not have been possible without the help of the many generous citizens of McDuffie County who willingly and gratefully trusted me with their pictures for this purpose. I am indebted to them for their generosity and faith. Unfortunately, the histories of many of our landmarks and people have been lost because there are no pictures of them. As Edith H. Roth stated when asked if she had a picture of her grandfather's livery stable in downtown Thomson, "The picture is only in my memory."

It is my hope that the whole community can now enjoy the intriguing history of McDuffie County through the photographs compiled in this book, thanks to those who have shared their photographs for this purpose. Although there are many individuals listed in the captions to whom I owe gratitude, I would specifically like to thank the City of Thomson, McDuffie County, William Dunn Wansley, Rusty Lovelace, and the McDuffie Museum for their help and large contributions of images. My only regret is that I did not have the time or space to include more.

While working on this project, I gained a deeper understanding of the fact that what we do today will affect tomorrow. The images in this book are evidence that the people and places of yesterday paved the way for the present. As we marvel at the past today, our descendants will do the same of us in the future. This year, we commemorate the 150th anniversary of McDuffie County. Let us look forward to the future that we are presently creating and strive to work together for progress and harmony in our community.

INTRODUCTION

McDuffie County was formed by an act of the Georgia General Assembly on October 18, 1870, from portions of Warren and Columbia Counties. Although some were against the idea of a new county, citizens in both counties felt that forming a new county would better serve the citizens in this area. During the time of the creation of the new county, those wishing to do business in town would have had a great distance to travel, by horse, to the nearest county seat. Creating smaller counties was a common practice across the state of Georgia so that citizens could do business at the county seat and return home in one day.

The majority of McDuffie County is made up of land that was ceded by Native Americans in 1763. McDuffie County is part of a region that was formerly called St. Paul's Parish under the British colonial government. McDuffie County was formed from parts of eastern Warren County and western Columbia County in 1870. It is recorded in *A History of McDuffie County* that the portion of McDuffie County gained from Warren County was originally a portion of Wilkes County, part of land that was ceded by Native Americans in 1773, and the portion taken from Columbia County was once part of Richmond County, before the creation of Columbia County in 1790.

McDuffie County is known for being home of the Quaker community Wrightsboro, which predates the county. There are two incorporated areas in McDuffie County: the city of Thomson, which has served as the county seat since the creation of the county, and the town of Dearing, located in the southern portion of the county. Other notable communities mentioned on past maps are Boneville, Raysville, Mesena, Cobbham, Scuffletown, Autney, Lombardy, Saw Dust, Mount Pleasant, and Hamilton's Crossroads.

McDuffie County has reared many notable citizens who are recognized nationally and worldwide. A few of the more widely known are Sen. Thomas Edward Watson, blues legend Blind Willie McTell, football greats Eddie Lee Ivery and Ray Guy, and Rev. Romulus Moore, a state legislator who served during the Reconstruction era.

Today, McDuffie is a thriving county with seven public schools, a technical college, numerous churches, many locally owned businesses, agricultural production, several large corporations, industry, access to Interstate 20, and a portion of Fort Gordon in its southern tip.

One

Forming a New County

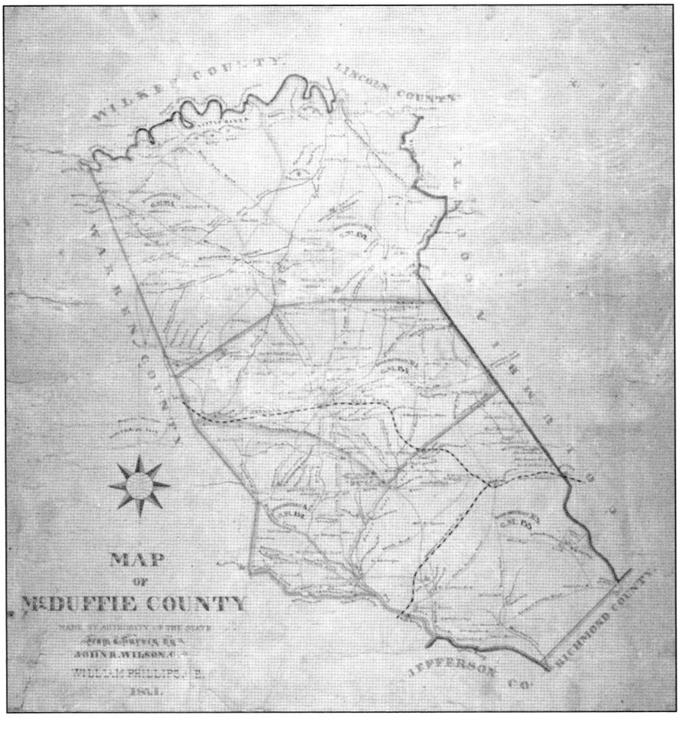

This map shows McDuffie County's original boundaries, roads, and property owners in a survey completed by Col. John Wilson, county surveyor, in 1871 shortly after the creation of the new county. McDuffie County was created by taking portions of eastern Warren County and western Columbia County. At the time of its creation, Georgians preferred to be able to make it to their county seat and back home in one day. Before the creation of McDuffie County, this would have been impossible traveling by horse on poorly maintained roads. (Courtesy of William Dunn Wansley.)

McDuffie County's namesake was George McDuffie, a senator, representative, and governor in South Carolina. At the time of his birth, the family's home was in the part of Columbia County that is now McDuffie County. McDuffie's birthplace, on George McDuffie Road, is marked with a historical marker. (Courtesy of Lewis Smith.)

J. Edgar Thomson, surveyor for the Georgia Railroad, was originally from Philadelphia but spent time in McDuffie County constructing the railroad that traverses through the heart of Thomson. The city of Thomson, flourishing with growth from the railroad, is named after him. Local historian Lewis Smith published a detailed biography of Smith titled *J. Edgar Thomson, the Georgia Rail Road Years, 1833–1845.* (Courtesy of Lewis Smith.)

Pictured is the historic McDuffie County Courthouse in its original splendor. The deed for the courthouse was secured on February 8, 1872, and the building was dedicated at a public program on December 8, 1873. Renovations to the original courthouse were completed in 1930 and 1970. The 1970 renovation included significant additions. The courthouse was used for government affairs until the completion of the new Thomson–McDuffie County Government Complex in 2011. (Courtesy of the McDuffie County Board of Commissioners.)

Thomson, previously known as "Hickory Level," "the Slashes," and "Frog Pond," grew up around the railroad on the farm land of John Langston. The bustling little country town was chosen as the county seat at the formation of McDuffie County. This photograph shows life at Thomson's depot around the turn of the 20th century. (Courtesy of Murray Boyd Beckum.)

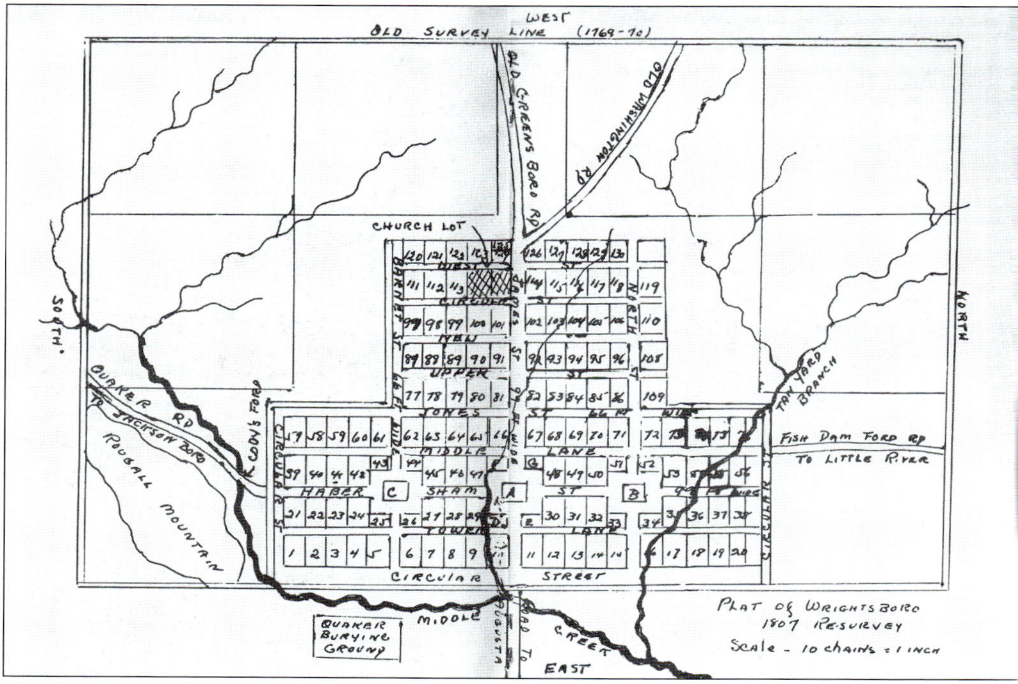

The historic Wrightsboro community predates the United States and is named after Georgia's royal governor James Wright, who granted Quakers from North Carolina and Pennsylvania thousands of acres in present-day McDuffie County. The settlement provided a buffer between the town of Augusta and Native Americans to the west. Although many of the Quaker settlers dispersed after the American Revolution, some stayed. Many of the citizens of McDuffie County are descendants of the original Quaker families. (Courtesy of Pearl Baker.)

Named after Capt. Thomas Cobb of the Revolutionary War, the small village of Cobbham was on the border between McDuffie and Columbia Counties. This photograph, taken around 1920, shows a group riding at the Dunn Farm. Sarah Louise Dunn Gibson is on the second horse from the left. (Courtesy of William Dunn Wansley.)

Pictured is the Dearing Depot. (Courtesy of the Thomson–McDuffie County Library.)

Boneville, in the southeastern portion of McDuffie County, was named after Jones Bones and was first called Bonesville. This was the previous site of an old mill, a large antebellum house, a post office, a church, and a one-room schoolhouse. People from the surrounding area, particularly Augusta, would take the railroad to Boneville to visit the Dixie Inn, a popular vacation and recreation spot in the early 20th century. Pictured is the Boneville Post Office, which was established in September 1884 and is still standing. (Courtesy of the McDuffie County Historic Preservation Commission.)

According to the *McDuffie Weekly Journal*, at the time of his death in November 1884, Hillary Langford, left, was the oldest citizen, at 91 years old, and had 278 descendants. Langford is buried at Salem United Methodist Church. Col. John R. Wilson, right, was the first county surveyor for McDuffie County. Langford and Wilson, along with a few others, were part of the original crew that surveyed McDuffie County. (Courtesy of the McDuffie County Board of Commissioners.)

A large crowd is standing outside the Thomson Depot for an educational exhibit in 1908. The building behind the train is the old Eureka Hotel, or Langston Hotel. This was the home of John Langston. Before the railroad was constructed, he owned a large amount of land in the current downtown Thomson area. The home was added on to and used as a hotel for those passing through Thomson. (Courtesy of Murray Boyd Beckum.)

This photograph of the Thomson Depot shows the old Masonic lodge in the background with decorative brickwork at the top. The building has been modified but is still standing on Railroad Street. (Courtesy of Murray Boyd Beckum.)

The historic Rock House is the oldest surviving stone residence in Georgia. Part of the historic Quaker community Wrightsboro, the house was built by Thomas Ansley in 1875 on the 4,700 acres he received from land grants. Pres. Jimmy Carter, as well as many from McDuffie County, descend from Thomas Ansley. (Courtesy of the McDuffie Museum.)

Pictured are Sen. Thomas "Tom" Edward Watson and his wife, Georgia Durham Watson, at Hickory Hill. Tom Watson, born near Thomson, descended from the original Quaker families that settled in McDuffie County. He was elected to the Georgia legislature, US House of Representatives, and US Senate, and was a presidential nominee for the People's Party in 1904. (Courtesy of the McDuffie Museum.)

Standing outside of the McDuffie County Courthouse are, from left to right, McDuffie County officials R.H. Pearce, clerk of superior court; I.G. Worrill, tax collector; C.H. Ellington, ordinary; and Shade Hawes, sheriff. (Courtesy of John McBrayer.)

Two

PEOPLE OF THE PAST

Col. Thomas Carr (1758–1820) was a Revolutionary War soldier, "Yazooist," Georgia legislator, and builder of the Alexandria Establishment between 1803 and 1806. (Courtesy of William Dunn Wansley.)

Mary Hart Adkins (1831–1893) was the daughter of Baptist minister Rev. Aaron Adkins. She was born and lived most of her life in what is now McDuffie County. She was the wife of Dr. Cicero Gibson and the mother of six sons, four of whom became medical doctors. One became a dentist, and the other became a lawyer. She was a direct descendant of the original Quaker Hart, Lowe, Moore, and Mooney families who settled Wrightsboro, Georgia, in 1768. (Courtesy of William Dunn Wansley.)

This picture shows Gen. Stephen Drane (left) and Col. John R. Wilson. This is one of several similar images of men with surveying tools. They are suspected to be members of the original surveying crew of McDuffie County in 1870. The map they produced is shown on page 19. (Courtesy of the McDuffie County Board of Commissioners.)

Rev. Thomas Butler West (pictured) was the progenitor of the West family of McDuffie County. He was the first pastor of Thomson Baptist Church and built the grand house that once sat on the triangle lot between Mesena Road and Tom Watson Way (formerly Lumpkin Street). Reverend West's son Col. John T. West, a lawyer known throughout the state, was killed in a hunting accident on the "Old West Farm." West View Cemetery is named for him. (Courtesy of First Baptist Church of Thomson.)

Dr. Cicero Sterling Gibson (1825–1883) was born in Warren County, Georgia, to Thomas and Mary Gardner Gibson. He graduated from the Medical College at Augusta in 1848 and practiced medicine for several years in Tennille, Georgia, then moved to the Adkins home on Brier Creek in McDuffie County. (Courtesy of William Dunn Wansley.)

Pictured are the Gibson brothers of Brier Creek. From left to right are dentist Dr. Thomas Crawford Gibson (1854–1941), Dr. Sterling Gibson (1858–1926), Dr. William Aaron Gibson Sr. (1852–1918), Dr. Cicero Gibson Jr. (1866–1937), and attorney John Gibson (1865–1942). Not pictured is Dr. Isaac Adkins Gibson (1861–1928). The photograph is believed to have been taken in April 1883 at the funeral of their father, Dr. Cicero Gibson Sr. (Courtesy of William Dunn Wansley.)

Ansley family members pictured here are, from left to right, Floyd, Thomas "Enos," Thelma, Milton, and Myrtle. Enos Ansley was a descendant of Thomas Ansley, builder of the Rock House in 1785. He and his wife, Myrtle, made their home in White Oak near the border of McDuffie and Columbia Counties. (Courtesy of the Ansley family.)

The Ellington family is pictured in the summer of 1904 on the front steps of their home, which was once on a large farm but is now inside the city of Thomson on Gordon Street. It is now Thomson Funeral System. Clarence Hutchens "C.H." Ellington served in the state senate from 1890 to 1891 and was the county ordinary from 1898 to 1909. From left to right are (first row) Emily Edith Ellington, C.H. Ellington with Eva Ellington Walker, Margaret Pearce Bennett Ellington with Sara Eugenia Ellington, and Arthur George Ellington; (second row) Margaret Clare Ellington Gasque, Carl Henry Ellington, Claude Bennett Ellington, Marie Lamkin Ellington (Carl's wife), and Eugenia Pearce Bennett. In the background at right is Jack Parks, the family's cook, and the woman in the left background is his wife. (Courtesy of the McDuffie County Clerk of Superior Court's Office.)

This family portrait includes, from left to right, (first row) John Edward Smith, Henslee Smith, and Vera Claire Smith; (second row) Baxter Fenelon Smith, Evelyn Smith, and Clara Henslee Smith. The photograph was taken on June 21, 1906. (Courtesy of Bunnie Hall Walden.)

This portrait taken on December 14, 1901, shows the children of William Owen Harrison and Cora Wilson Harrison. From left to right are (first row) L.M. and Bernard; (second row) Walter, Jim, and Kate. Not pictured is Miriam Harrison. (Courtesy of Edith Harrison Roth.)

Dr. Cicero Gibson was the first person in McDuffie County to own an automobile. He is pictured here in downtown Thomson. (Courtesy of Stacy Turner.)

Forrest Beckum and Pace McCorkle are standing in front of the wrought iron fence that surrounded the historic McDuffie County Courthouse on Main Street in 1922. (Courtesy of Murray Boyd Beckum.)

Dr. William Pitts and his family are pictured outside their home, which was formerly on Jackson Street and later moved to Salem Road. Dr. Pitts was a leader in the formation of First Bapti Church in Thomson and practiced medicine in McDuffie County, developing and bottling h own medicines. (Courtesy of First Baptist Church of Thomson.)

Pictured in 1954 are some members of Thomson's five garden clubs. They are, from left to righ (first row) Betty Howell, Mildred Adams Russell, and Mrs. D.M. Hutcheson; (second row) Marj Mobley, Myrtle Perryman, Grace Poss, Mary A. Brown, Mrs. Robert L. Harrison, and Mrs. Joh Adams. (Courtesy of the City of Thomson.)

William Owen Harrison and Cora Wilson Harrison owned and lived in Sen. Tom Watson's home, named Hickory Hill by Watson, prior to Watson purchasing the Wilson estate. (Courtesy of Edith Harrison Roth.)

From left to right, city clerk Floyd Montgomery, unidentified, and fire truck driver Watt Baston stand in front of the old Thomson Fire Department's fire engine on Main Street. The Hall house (left) and Turner house can be seen in the background. (Courtesy of Jimmy Crawley.)

Pictured here are, from left to right, Walter Harrison, Marian Howell, Miriam Harrison, Kate Harrison Lowe, and Bob Howell. Marian Howell was the mother of John Gross Howell, owner of the Nehi Bottling Company on Hendricks Street across from the Thomson Depot. (Courtesy of Edith Harrison Roth.)

This photograph, taken December 6, 1976, at the annual Christmas party of Judge Randall Evans Jr., includes William A. Evans, Augusta; Harvey J. Kennedy, Barnesville; Judge Randall Evans Jr. Thomson; Bobby Lee Cook Sr., Summerville; C.W. "Red" Herndon, Thomson; J.C. Thornton Thomson; Howard L. "Sack" Buffington, Mesena; Harry "Colonel Sanders" Camp, Dearing; Carl Powers, Thomson; and William W. Lavigno Sr., Dearing. (Courtesy of the McDuffie Museum.)

Marshall Wellborn Dunn (1855–1944) and Mattie Neal (1872–1958) are pictured in their wedding photograph in June 1903. Dunn was one of the leading merchants of Thomson and served for a number of years as the McDuffie County superintendent of schools. He is buried at the Thomson City Cemetery. (Courtesy of William Dunn Wansley.)

From left to right, Margaret Knox, Sterling Gibson Jr., Louise Dunn, and Ben O'Neal are seated on the running board of an automobile in 1915. (Courtesy of William Dunn Wansley.)

Dr. William Aaron Gibson Jr. and Sarah Louise Dunn Gibson are pictured in 1923. They were married at the First United Methodist Church in Thomson in Ma of that year. (Courtesy of William Dunn Wansley.)

Judge J.C. Dunn, a native of McDuffie County, was a prominent planter and merchant who owned a store at Cobbham and was the sole commissioner, and later ordinary, in McDuffie County from 1933 to 1949. Dunn was part owner of McDuffie County's newspaper, the *McDuffie Progress*. When he passed away in 1954, he was serving as the secretary of the Georgia State Board of Corrections. (Courtesy of William Dunn Wansley.)

Dr. William Aaron Gibson Sr. (left) and Charlie Kitchens are pictured in 1880. (Courtesy of William Dunn Wansley.)

The board of directors are pictured at the ground-breaking ceremony for the First National Bank on Jackson Street in 1965. From left to right are Bill Leverett (president), Hodges Mobley, Jones Arnold, Jim Usry, Paul Bowden (chairman), Johnny McNeill, Pearl Kunnes, Stacy Turner, L.D. "Pop" Berry, and an unidentified architect. (Courtesy of Stacy Turner.)

Children of the Smith family stand in front of the wrought iron fence that once surrounded the historic McDuffie County Courthouse and the Thomson First United Methodist Church. (Courtesy of Bunnie Hall Walden.)

John Edward Smith was a prominent landowner, farmer, and businessman of McDuffie County. He was president of the Bank of Thomson and owner of Smith Manufacturing Co. (a large cotton mill), and represented the county in the legislature from 1905 to 1906. A stained-glass window at the First United Methodist Church in Thomson commemorates his generosity to the church. (Courtesy of Bunnie Hall Walden.)

People wait patiently on the last day of operation, Saturday, August 3, 1963, at the old Bank of Thomson at 811 Main Street. A new bank was constructed on the corner of Main and White Oak Streets. (Courtesy of Murray Boyd Beckum.)

Shelton Asbury "S.A." Blanchard, left, pictured with brother in law Clarence Foster Jr. and Clarence "Rudy" Foster III, owned and operated the Blanchard Funeral Home in Thomson for many years. After Blanchard's death, Clarence Foster Jr. continued the funeral operation with the help of his son Rudy. (Courtesy of Harriett Dozier Reeves.)

Blacksmith R.G. Story and his wife, Cora Story, stand in front of their home on the corner of Gordon Street and Ellington Avenue in Thomson in the early 1900s. They had 12 children: Marie Story Mauldin, Frank Story, Louise Story Pearson, James Story, Georgia Elizabeth Story, Hubert Story, Merle Story Colvin, Vannie Story Wall, Mary Story Waller, Radford Story, and two who died as infants. (Courtesy of Jennifer Whitaker Newton.)

Lloyd Hanson is in the driver's seat of his Coca-Cola delivery truck with sons Charles T. Hanson Sr. (left) and Barry Hanson standing in front. This picture was taken about 1951. The Coca-Cola bottling works building was on Greenway Street in Thomson and now houses the senior citizens center. (Courtesy of JoAnne Parris Hanson.)

Roy Lovelace Sr. and Pearl Lovelace pose outside their home on White Oak Street in 1921. (Courtesy of Rusty Lovelace.)

The Wilson brothers, James, John, and Bob, are pictured with their mother, Norma Watson Wilson. The brothers owned and operated several successful McDuffie County businesses, including the McDuffie Oil and Fertilizer Company (MOFCO), Wilson Furniture Company, the Cotton Patch Motel, the Wilson Motor Company (a Ford dealership), the Wilson Company (a real estate agency), and Wilson Homes. James Wilson Jr., along with his sons, built and operated the White Columns Inn. (Courtesy of Cindy Wilson.)

Children of the Wilson family gather around the table for a meal inside the Wilson family's home on Augusta Highway. In 1935, James Edgar Wilson Sr. and Norma Watson Wilson built the home on the site of an earlier one. The John S. Watson home was moved when the Wilson family built its two-story brick home in 1935. Members of the Wilson family still own and occupy the home on the family farm, Pine Top. (Courtesy of Cindy Wilson.)

Bob, James "Boots," and John Wilson are pictured with their father, James E. Wilson Sr. (Courtesy of Cindy Wilson.)

Gordon Arrington Sr. stands outside his service station on Highway 278. Arrington's Service Station, originally known as Ray's Service Station, was purchased by Arrington in the early 1970s. He sold clothes, ammunition, food, and gas, as well as real estate. All three of his children, Gordon "Gordy" Arrington Jr., Freddy Arrington, and Debbie Arrington Gunn, were employed in the family business. (Courtesy of Debbie Arrington Gunn.)

McDuffie County officials gather on the courthouse steps on July 28, 1967. From left to right are W.C. "Top" Watson, clerk of court; Myrtis McCorkle, tax collector; Forrest Prather, county commissioner; Winton Adams, county commission chairman; Romie Powell, county commissioner; John "Bubba" Watson, ordinary; and William Swan, sheriff. (Courtesy of the McDuffie Museum.)

Emily Edith Ellington (1892–1961), daughter of C.H. Ellington, was a prominent member of the First Baptist Church of Thomson, teaching the young men's Bible class for over 40 years. She also served as an English teacher in McDuffie County for many years. (Courtesy of First Baptist Church of Thomson.)

The women of Thomson's home demonstration program pose in 1954. From left to right are Mrs. Henry Ansley, Mrs. Will Shields, Mrs. Cleve Jones, Mrs. Farris Morris, and Genevieve Creasy, home demonstration agent. (Courtesy of the City of Thomson.)

Two men sit outside a store in downtown Thomson in the late 1930s. (Courtesy of William Dunn Wansley.)

Sarah Louise Dunn Gibson (left) walks the sidewalks of downtown Thomson. The truck beside her advertises Dozier's Electrical. (Courtesy of William Dunn Wansley.)

Judge J.C. Dunn looks up from the local newspaper inside Gibson's Drugstore. (Courtesy of William Dunn Wansley.)

Sarah Louise Dunn Gibson is standing outside Gibson's Drugstore with H.D. Everette in 1938. (Courtesy of William Dunn Wansley.)

Four generations of the Jones family pose in December 1971 on the Jones family farm. Eugene "Gene" Jones was a cattle farmer and fence installer. He and his wife, Phoebe Martin Jones, worked at Howell's grocery warehouse. From left to right are Gene Jones, James "Burr" Jones, and Clifford Jones holding Scott Jones. (Courtesy of Shirley Kelley Jones.)

Children of Robert Francis and Mary Arrington Kelley pose in the summer of 1916. From left to right are Pauline Mabel Kelley Wood Simons, Arthur "Theodore" Kelley, Horace Buford "Doc" Kelley, and Annie Lee Phillips Cason. (Courtesy of Shirley Kelley Jones.)

Sarah Hardwick Calhoun is pressing sugarcane to make syrup on the Calhoun farm in McDuffie County. Her brother Saul Hardwick was McDuffie County's first black mortician. Her husband, Vennie, was a farmer, mason, and a deacon of his church. Travelers along Interstate 20 would purchase the Calhouns' syrup. (Courtesy of Wayne Calhoun.)

Vennie and Sarah Calhoun are making syrup on their farm. Vennie Calhoun's father, Cato Calhoun, a freed slave of the family of Vice Pres. John C. Calhoun, came to this area from South Carolina to reunite with his mother after the Civil War in 1867. Cato lived on the Printup farm in Dearing and worked as a sharecropper in the early 1900s. Vennie's sister Viola Calhoun Avery was a well-known educator who traveled to various country schoolhouses, educating young African Americans. Viola Avery Street in the city of Thomson bears her name. (Courtesy of Wayne Calhoun.)

From left to right, Wallace Whitaker, Joe Bailey, Billie Reuben Printup, Earl Printup, Jap Miles, and Eugene Bailey of the Dearing Motorcycle Club are pictured in front of the hill just north of the railroad track in Dearing in 1915. (Courtesy of Sean Kelley.)

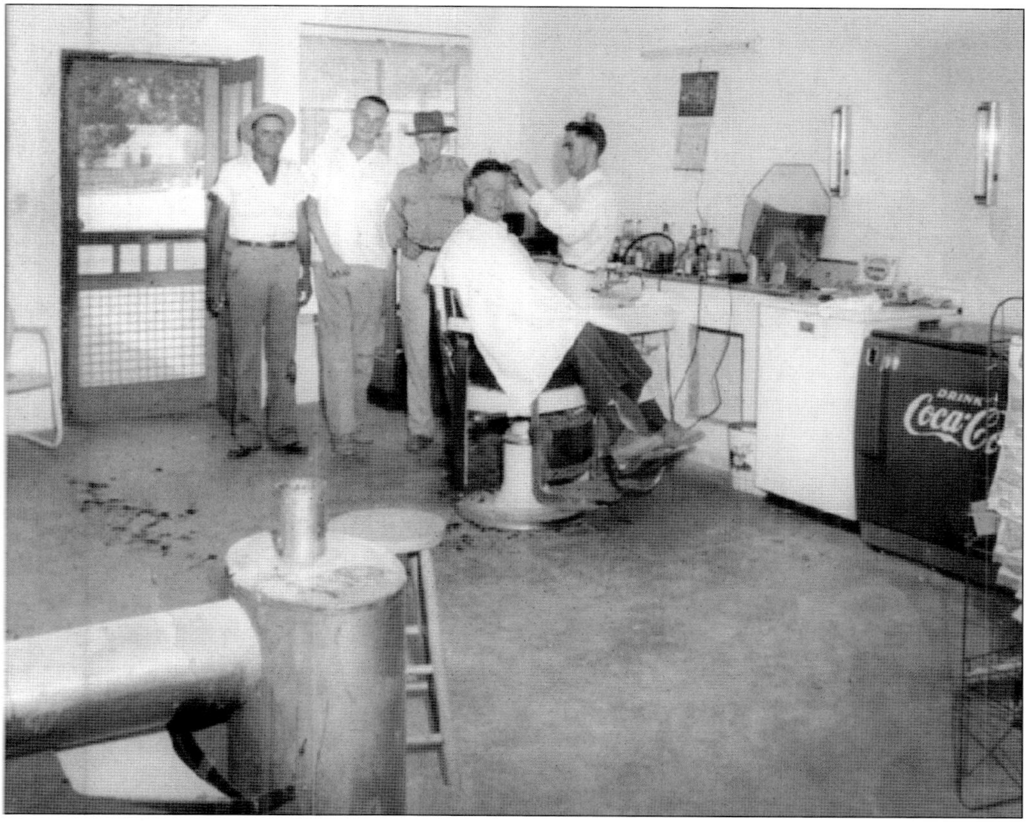

From left to right, Calvin Neal, Sammie Kelley, and Jimmy Taylor are standing beside Ralph McCorkle as he cuts Jimbo Welch's hair in a Dearing barbershop. (Courtesy of Sean Kelley.)

Jack Usry is making cane syrup on the Usry farm in the 1940s. (Courtesy of Sean Kelley.)

Allene Reeves is pictured outside her sandwich shop on Augusta Highway in Dearing. Reeves Sandwich Shop began in the 1940s when Jerry Reeves purchased the building from Itie Edwards for $1,000. He and his wife, Allene, operated the popular sandwich shop until 1984. "Miss Allene," known for her tasty hamburgers, retired at age 76. (Courtesy of Sean Kelley.)

Officers of the Thomson Fire Department pose at the old fire station on Main Street. From left to right are (first row) Hubert Echols, Billy Smith, and Warren Sims; (second row) Bo Teston, Bub Crawley, J.D. Mathews, and George Poss. (Courtesy of Jimmy Crawley.)

Vinnie Williams, left, and First Lady Rosalynn Carter, wife of Pres. Jimmy Carter, admire a flower on the Carters' tour of the historic Rock House in McDuffie County. President Carter is a descendant of Thomas Ansley, builder of Georgia's oldest stone dwelling. (Courtesy of Rusty Lovelace.)

The Knox Homes Corporation started from an earlier business known as Knox Building Supply on Railroad Street in Thomson. The Knox brothers, pictured in front of a Knox Homes advertisement and half-assembled home are, from left to right, Wyck, Robert, Pete, and Lawrence. They grew the family business with Knox Homes, which built prefabricated houses. Pete was the driving force, and he and Wyck largely operated the business. Lawrence Knox worked at the wood plant, and Robert "Bob" Knox Sr. served as the company's attorney. (Courtesy of the McDuffie Museum.)

Henry Jones is standing behind a counter full of handmade shoes in his shoe store on Journal Street in Thomson. (Courtesy of Bill Shields.)

Sarah Louise Fluker started in education in a one-room schoolhouse in McDuffie County. In her 61-year career, she taught about 7,500 to 8,000 students. In 1948, Fluker was elected McDuffie County school superintendent, a significant achievement for a woman at that time. In addition to local endeavors, she introduced the Minimum Foundation Program of Education, upgrading Georgia's schools and improving teacher benefits. (Courtesy of the Fluker family.)

This 1916 photograph shows Howell (left) and John Hunt. The Hunt children were reared in the Wrightsboro community near Wrightsboro Methodist Church. (Courtesy of Suzanne Hunt Green.)

Marcus Culpepper Sr. and Jessie Montgomery Culpepper had two children, Marcus Culpepper Jr. and Anne Culpepper Eubank. Marcus Culpepper Sr. started Culpepper Lumber Company in Dearing, Georgia. Later, Marcus Culpepper Jr. opened a Culpepper Lumber Company location in Thomson in 1953. (Courtesy of Marcia Hardin Culpepper Harden.)

Jessie Montgomery Culpepper is pictured around 1953 with her three grandchildren, Peggy Eubank Brooks, Marcia Culpepper Harden, and Harold Eubank. (Courtesy of Marcia Hardin Culpepper Harden.)

The children of John and Essie (Tudor) Phillips of Iron Hill Road in Dearing are pictured here. From left to right are Willie, Gene, Jack, Dovie, Doris, Howard, John D., Ida Belle, Bennie, and James. (Courtesy of Robin Wheelbarger Johnson.)

This turn-of-the-20th-century photograph shows a steam fire engine of the Thomson Fire Department. (Courtesy of Rusty Lovelace.)

Amanda Wilson Hawes, wife of Dr. Ellington Cody Hawes, is sitting on the front porch of the West house, between Mesena and Cedar Rock Roads. Her daughter Laura Hawes West was married to John T. West. Amanda was the granddaughter of Capt. John Wilson, a Revolutionary War veteran for whom the local Daughters of the American Revolution chapter is named. (Courtesy of John McBrayer.)

Men are transporting Tom Watson's library to the Thomson Depot from Hickory Hill. The man at far left, seated on top of the wagon, is Harley Alexander Parris. Watson's brother William is standing to the right beside the wagon. (Courtesy of Rusty Lovelace.)

These women served as escorts for the Thomson Company, one of McDuffie County's largest employers. (Courtesy of Rusty Lovelace.)

This photograph was taken at the McDuffie County Hospital's 10th anniversary in 1962. Seated from left to right are Mrs. Lambert, Mrs. Haddon, and Mrs. Pearl Usry. Standing in unknown order are Inez Lemke, Forest McGahee, Leonard Turner, Mrs. Graves, Dave McNeill Jr., Lawrence Knox (chairman), Joe Usry (administrator), Bill Leverett, H.H. Bonner, Hodges T. Mobley, and Jim F. Usry. (Courtesy of Rusty Lovelace.)

Bob Knox Sr., surrey master, and Anne Brown, wife of Walter Brown, are seen at the Belle Meade Hunt. At the time of the Belle Meade Hunt's beginning, Bob Knox Sr. managed the land he and his three brothers inherited from their father, Peter Knox. The brothers graciously permitted the use of the Knox lands near Wrightsboro for the hunt. (Courtesy of Luckey Printing.)

From left to right, Charles "Wormy" Newton III, James Wilson, and John McNeill Jr. are pictured at the Belle Meade Hunt. Wilson organized the Belle Meade Hunt, which began in 1966. (Courtesy of Luckey Printing.)

Three

McDuffie County Churches

The First Baptist Church was organized by seven members who began meeting in the home of Dr. William Pitts in the village of Thomson on November 14, 1859. Members previously worshipped at Sweetwater Baptist Church but felt there was a need for a Baptist church in the growing community of Thomson. The first church building was erected in 1860. The current brick sanctuary building was constructed and first used in 1909 but was not dedicated until the note was paid off in 1916. This image shows the exterior before the renovations and additions of 1954. (Courtesy of First Baptist Church of Thomson.)

This was the inside of the First Baptist Church of Thomson before extensive changes were mad during the enlargement of 1954. The sanctuary, originally square-shaped, was enlarged to its curren rectangular design to seat more congregants for the growing Baptist church. The enlargemen altered the baptistery, alcove, and seating arrangement. This photograph shows the decoration for the wedding of Dr. Weldon and Frances Neal on March 27, 1931, at noon. (Courtesy of Firs Baptist Church of Thomson.)

The First United Methodist Church began one mile north of the present site on Washington Road at the location of the small wooden Bethany Church. James R. Wilson exchanged property with Bethany Church. The first church at the current site was a wooden building, but in 1902, the present brick sanctuary was built. The beautiful stained-glass windows honor the memory of Mr. and Mrs. John E. Smith, who gave generously for the erection of the new building. In 1946–1947, the church annex was constructed, including the Knox Chapel, which was given in memory of Peter S. and Gertrude Austin Knox and Hattie Emily Knox by the Knox family. (Courtesy of First United Methodist Church.)

Presbyterians began meeting at the home of Lula Farmer as early as 1916. Because of World War I, the group's efforts ceased. In 1938, two sisters, Agnes Boswell and Leila McCommons, led a new effort to start a Presbyterian church in Thomson. A young ministerial student from Augusta, Samuel Hollingsworth Zealy, began holding church meetings at the community building on August 7, 1938. In 1941, the church purchased and renovated a building on Lumpkin Street behind the Laura Jones Elementary School from Hattie Belle Martin for $2,200. In April 1948, the church purchased a 300-by-400-foot lot from the Johnson Turner subdivision for $2,000. The current church building, designed by Scroggs & Ewing of Augusta, was completed in 1949 by local contractor L.N. Crawley. The first services in the new church on Jackson Street were held on Sunday, October 2, 1949. (Courtesy of Thomson Presbyterian Church.)

Springfield Baptist Church was formed in November 1873. The congregation first met in the former Columbia Institute school building. The church seen here was built after 1883. After 1940, an annex was constructed along with an educational building, and the brick veneer seen here was added. (Courtesy of Springfield Baptist Church.)

Residents in the Pine Grove Church area worshipped at Union Church until 1827, when they decided to begin holding services in their own community. In 1830, a total of 2.7 acres were acquired for the Pine Grove Meetinghouse from Adam Scott and George Darsey. In 1963, the church took out a loan to brick the sanctuary, add Sunday school rooms, restrooms, and a baptistery. In 1976, the family of P.S. Knox Jr. donated the house across from the church on Washington Road for use as a pastorium. In 1979, the steeple was donated by the Edmunds family in memory of Lilla Edmunds. Later that year, the fellowship hall was constructed. (Courtesy of Frances Darden.)

In 1869, Mount Pleasant Baptist Church was organized through the help of members of Sweetwater Baptist Church on land donated by Brother Jim Norris. Rev. Tom West of Sweetwater Baptist Church and several deacons contributed funds, along with Rev. Mike Wilson, Deacon Daniel Showers, and Brother Danford Wilson. The congregation saw large growth during the mid-2000s, and a new church was built. The old building was renovated for a fellowship hall. (Courtesy of Rosa Lazenby Hunt.)

Meetings of the Salem United Methodist Church were first held at Piney Wood Schoolhouse in 1820. Because of growth, the congregants decided to build a church in the community. Members cut trees, took them to the sawmill, and brought lumber back to the church yard to stack and dry. The church was completed in 1822. In 1960, an old house was purchased from Southern Bell for $1 to be used for a Sunday school building. (Courtesy of Roger Whitaker.)

Sweetwater Baptist Church was organized on October 11, 1802, and is one of the oldest churches in McDuffie County. Sweetwater helped in the formation of several sister Baptist churches, including the First Baptist Church in Thomson, Marshall Baptist Church, and Fort Creek Baptist Church. This is the original wooden building. The sanctuary has been rebuilt numerous times due to fires. (Courtesy of Sammy Luckey.)

Sweetwater Baptist Church members are shown in the Thomson High School auditorium after the church sanctuary burned in the 1960s. (Courtesy of Sammy Luckey.)

The McDuffie County Fire Department is on the scene of a fire that left Sweetwater Baptist Church in ruins in 1970. (Courtesy of Sammy Luckey.)

From left to right, Verne Ogletree, Sunday school superintendent; Gene Luke, deacon chairman; Gene Heirs, pastor; and David Clabo, music minister, survey the smoldering ruins of Sweetwater Baptist Church in 1970. (Courtesy of Sammy Luckey.)

This was the congregation inside Sweetwater Baptist Church one Sunday morning during service in the 1950s. (Courtesy of Jennifer Whitaker Newton.)

Marshall Baptist Church was near the old White Oak Campground in McDuffie County on Marshall Church Road. On January 16, 1877, John T. May donated six acres for a church and cemetery. The original members were Stockston family members from Union Baptist Church, May, Dougherty, Johnson, Wade, McGahee, Whitaker, and Blanchard from Sweetwater Baptist Church, Reid family members from Thomson Baptist Church, and Eliza J. Samuels from Sharon Baptist Church. The wooden church pictured here burned on July 2, 1973, and a new brick building was constructed and dedicated on March 17, 1974. (Courtesy of Marshall Baptist Church.)

Vanderhorst Christian Methodist Episcopal Church is nearing completion in 1954. The church began in 1884, named for Bishop Richard Vanderhorst. The first known building was on a lot purchased from B.F. Johnson, bounded by Dublin and Railroad Streets in Thomson. This church was destroyed by fire on March 16, 1952. The congregation met in the McDuffie County Training School, Springfield Baptist Church, and Paupers Aid Society until the new church was constructed. On June 9, 1952, the church purchased land from Nellie Lowe on Washington Road and held the first service at the current location on May 14, 1953. (Courtesy of City of Thomson.)

Flint Hill Baptist Church was in northern McDuffie County near Wilkes County. It was founded in 1874 by Rev. J.A. Shank. Prior to the church being constructed, members met inside the Griffin home. In the photograph are Lon Griffin, Mr. and Mrs. Jessie Morris, Mr. and Mrs. Joe Porter, Fannie Griffin, Mr. and Mrs. Jim Griffin, Mr. Frons Strother and daughter Lilly, Mary Paschal, Mr. Loy Bradley, Almeta Sistrunk, Mrs. William Davey, Rev. Joe Shank, Mr. and Mrs. Arthur Porter, Mr. Rufus Shank, and Mr. and Mrs. Charlie Woodall. (Courtesy of Louisa Hickman.)

The Boneville Methodist Church was built in 1902 on land donated by M.W. Fuller and his daughter Bessie Fuller Rogers. The church added Sunday school rooms and a fellowship hall in 1961. (Courtesy of the McDuffie County Historic Preservation Commission.)

David McGahee deeded land to the trustees of Fort Creek Baptist Church on April 10, 1860. The original trustees were F.M. Hobbs, Samuel McGahee, and William Printup. The first church was a one-room building valued at $600. It has seen many renovations and expansions. Because of growth, a new sanctuary was constructed in 2010 using some of the materials from the old building. (Courtesy of Shirley Kelley Jones.)

Members of the Kelley family pose outside Fort Creek Baptist Church after a family reunion. (Courtesy of Sammy Luckey.)

Union Church was organized in 1809 by those who had a desire to form a church in their own community. At that time, the nearest Baptist church was Sweetwater Baptist Church. The church's membership dwindled until finally closing in 1982. However, it was reopened and given new life by the Richards, Widener, and Pilgrim families in 1999 as Cornerstone Baptist Church. The church held services for the first time on Easter Sunday, April 4, 1999. The church voted to use the original name and discontinue using the name Cornerstone. Union Baptist Church now has an active congregation, and the sanctuary has been updated and restored. (Courtesy of Union Baptist Church.)

This was the inside of Union Baptist Church before members began renovating it. (Courtesy of Union Baptist Church.)

Wrightsboro Methodist Church, was built to serve people of all denominations in the Wrightsboro community. A committee requested title of the church building for the purposes of a Methodist Episcopal Church on February 9, 1877. The title was granted on April 11, 1879. (Courtesy of Suzanne Hunt Green.)

The Hunt family poses on the front steps of Wrightsboro Methodist Church around 1957. The family owned property in the Wrightsboro community and were members at Wrightsboro Methodist Church. Pictured are Bryan, Emma, Janice, Miriam, Sidney, Kathryn, Mae, Howell, Robert, Marsha, Gertrude, Nancy, Suzanne, Dixie, Ann, Claire, Jane, Barry, and Fay. (Courtesy of Suzanne Hunt Green.)

The Good Friday cross processional through downtown Thomson is a long-standing tradition. Area churches come together to carry a wooden cross through Thomson, symbolizing the journey of Jesus to his crucifixion. The image at left is from the 1970s. (Courtesy of First United Methodist Church.)

This photograph of ladies of the First United Methodist Church was taken before an event inside Knox Chapel. From left to right are (first row) unidentified, Mildred Wright, Vickie Howard, Ruth Wilson, and Pie Garrett; (second row) Pinkie Knox, Louise Gibson, Ruth Knox, Mary Lyles Knox, and Lucy Ray. (Courtesy of First United Methodist Church.)

Boy Scouts pose at First United Methodist Church during a ceremony to receive the God and Country award. From left to right are (first row) Jimmy Hall, Allan Hall, Rick Hawes, and Danny Johnson; (second row) Bob Wilson Jr., Tommy Lockett, Andy Knox, Tommy Dudley, Ben Willis, and Rev. John Maxwell. (Courtesy of First United Methodist Church.)

Pictured are members of the Girls in Action program at First Baptist Church in Thomson on March 24, 1947. Among those pictured are Ruth Anderson, Mr. and Mrs. F.A. Montgomery, Mrs. Jimmy Curtis, Mrs. M.W. Mosley, Marion Gross Howell, Dr. J. Pipkin, Leonard Lokey, Martha Lokey, Shirley Rabun, Carolyn Farr, Ludelle Langham, Pat Evans, Jackie Mann, Maxine Hunt, Laura Johnson, Ann Oster, Ruth Anderson, Joann Clary, Madelyn Farr, Gloria Gilland, Betty Ann Cason, Bert Johnson, and Grace Curtis. (Courtesy of First Baptist Church of Thomson.)

Members of Girls in Action pose at First Baptist Church in Thomson. (Courtesy of First Baptist Church.)

Ruth Anderson is crowned queen by Girls in Action leader Mrs. Jimmy Curtis on March 24, 1947. (Courtesy of First Baptist Church.)

These photographs were taken at White Oak Campground. Above, women stand outside what was described as a "tent." Below is a camp meeting in 1908. (Above, courtesy of Cindy Wilson; below, Courtesy of Edith Roth.)

The old White Oak Campground, originally in McDuffie County on White Oak Road, was deeded to the trustees of the Methodist Episcopal Church in 1832. During the Civil War, the campground ceased to be used for religious meetings. The new White Oak Campground was built in 1873 in Columbia County, just over the McDuffie County line. The original building committee for the tabernacle included many men from McDuffie County, and today many of the tents are owned by McDuffie residents. (Courtesy of the Thomson–McDuffie County Library.)

Green Branch Baptist Church was established on April 16, 1870. The first church was on US Army Corps of Engineers land near Flint Hill Baptist Church. The later building pictured here on Washington Highway has closed, and the congregants now hold services in Thomson. (Courtesy of the McDuffie Museum.)

Dearing Baptist Church was formed on September 19, 1912. The property for the church was donated by John R. Printup. He and his wife also donated to the building fund. (Courtesy of Sean Kelley.)

Dearing United Methodist Church was organized as the Dearing Methodist Episcopal Church by Rev. Thomas H. Gibson. The lot was donated by Jack Harris. (Courtesy of Sean Kelley.)

Adams Chapel Methodist Church is three miles east of Dearing. The lot was donated to the church by Benjamin Adams around 1896. (Courtesy of the McCommons and Stovall families.)

Silver Run Baptist Church, located in the southeastern tip of McDuffie County, was organized around 1800. (Courtesy of Sean Kelley.)

In January 1955, Ellen "Nellie" O'Shea McNeill donated a house on East Hall Street to be used for the first permanent Catholic church in Thomson. The parishioners renovated the building and converted it into a chapel. The church was named after McNeill's church in Chicago, Queen of Angels. (Courtesy of Queen of Angels Catholic Church.)

As the number of Catholics in the area grew, a larger church was needed. In 1967, six acres were purchased on Washington Road, and construction began. On May 19, 1968, the church and parish hall were dedicated. A rectory was added in 1984, and the religious education building was erected in 1986. (Courtesy of Louis Graziano.)

Four

McDuffie County Schools

The McDuffie County Board of Education building, at the corner of Main and Lee Streets, is pictured here. Prior to 1933, most schools were near or inside churches or in location central to large farming communities. School consolidation began in 1921, bringing the one-room schoolhouses and church schools to their end by 1933. A few of them are pictured in this chapter. The McDuffie County School System operates six schools: Thomson High School, Thomson-McDuffie Middle School, Norris Elementary School, Thomson Elementary School, J.A. Maxwell Elementary School, and Dearing Elementary School. (Courtesy of Luckey Printing.)

The Laura Jones School was previously the Thomson Grammar School. The Methodist church owned the land as early as 1873. The church trustees designated the land for educational purposes and a school, the Pierce Institute, named after Bishop George Pierce, was constructed. After the property was transferred to the city, this school building was erected in 1910. It housed all grades until 1929, when the first high school building was constructed on Main Street. Laura Jones School was conveyed back to the First United Methodist Church on September 15, 1989. The building was torn down to make way for the church's Family Life Center, which was consecrated in 1993. (Courtesy of First United Methodist Church.)

The first Thomson High School Building, constructed in 1929, was a one-story building boasting an ornate cupola. In 1938, the cupola was struck by lightning, and the building burned. The football stadium, also known as "the "Brickyard," was constructed out of the rubble from the previous high school, and a new high school building was constructed in the same place. The building pictured is the current school on Main Street, which served as Thomson High School until the construction of a new high school on White Oak Road in 1991. (Courtesy of Rusty Lovelace.)

This is an early photograph of the Thomson High School gymnasium. Its exterior has been modified since this time, and the gym is now one of the county's polling locations. (Courtesy of Rusty Lovelace.)

One of Thomson and McDuffie County's largest-known landmarks is the historic football stadium dubbed "the Brickyard." The large brick wall that surrounds the stadium was constructed using bricks from the high school building that burned in 1938. The Brickyard is across from the historic Thomson High School on Main Street and is still used as the football stadium. (Courtesy of Rusty Lovelace.)

J.A. Maxwell Elementary School has served students since 1977. Additional classrooms were added in 1983, 1986, and 1987. A major addition took place in 2002, adding eight classrooms and a new gymnasium. The school was named for James A. Maxwell, who served as McDuffie County school superintendent from 1953 to 1982. (Courtesy of Luckey Printing.)

Thomson Elementary School was constructed in 1954 with six classrooms, a lunchroom, and administrative offices. Additional classrooms, a media center, a gymnasium, and conference rooms have been added in 1957, 1961, 1967, 1987, 1998, 1999, and 2004. Thomson Elementary School currently houses second and third grades. (Courtesy of City of Thomson.)

McDuffie County Training School opened on Pine Street in 1936. In 1957, the school on Harrison Road known as R.L. Norris High School was opened and named McDuffie County Training School, and the building on Pine Street was renamed Pine Street School. In the late 1960s, the school was renamed Pine Street Elementary School. After desegregation, Pine Street Elementary served as an integrated elementary school for many years. (Courtesy of the Thomson–McDuffie County Library.)

A new Norris Elementary School stands on the site of the original R.L. Norris High School. The new school incorporated brick and hardwood flooring from the old high school. R.L. Norris High School served African American students from 1957 until 1970, when schools were desegregated. The original R.L. Norris High School is pictured here. The school's name pays homage to the longest-serving principal of McDuffie County Training School, Raymond Luther Norris. (Courtesy of the McDuffie Museum.)

The Thomson-McDuffie Junior High School was built in 2008 to accommodate eighth and ninth graders. After being open for two school years, ninth-grade students were moved back to Thomson High School, and this school has served as the Thomson-McDuffie Middle School since the fall of 2010. The school now houses grades six through eight. (Courtesy of the McDuffie County Board of Education.)

Due to growth of the school system, the new Thomson High School was built in 1991 and opened for classes in January 1992 on White Oak Road. (Courtesy of Luckey Printing.)

Pictured is Dearing Elementary School. (Courtesy of Luckey Printing.)

McDuffie County Training School principal S.M. Logan, who was also an agriculture teacher and band instructor, built the Center, an athletic building to serve African American students. He built apartments in the top for young black teachers to rent when moving to Thomson. The building was later used as the fieldhouse at the Brickyard before renovations to the stadium were completed. Principal Harris, who lived on West Street, also built apartments much later for young teachers to rent. (Courtesy of the Thomson–McDuffie County Library.)

The one-room schoolhouse in Boneville was constructed in 1903 and served students in the Boneville area. During the move toward consolidation, the school was closed in 1926. (Courtesy of the McDuffie County Historic Preservation Commission.)

Children of the Boneville School pose outside the old one-room schoolhouse for their yearly photograph. The school served children of all ages in the Boneville community. Unfortunately, all the children are unidentified except for William Marvin Parris Sr., seated at center in the first row. (Courtesy of Jo Ann Parris Hanson.)

Dearing High School was completed in the fall of 1938 and operated as the high school until the McDuffie County Board of Education voted to consolidate Dearing with Thomson High School in September 1959. (Courtesy of Sean Kelley.)

The Dearing Gymnasium is beside the old Dearing High School. (Courtesy of Sean Kelley.)

This was the Thomson High School student body in 1912. (Courtesy of William Dunn Wansley.

Pictured is the Thomson High School band in 1914. (Courtesy of William Dunn Wansley.)

The original Thomson High School was on Main Street where the historic Thomson High School building stands today. The original building, constructed in 1929, was one story with an ornate cupola on top. The cupola was struck by lightning in 1938, burning the school beyond repair. The historic "Brickyard" football stadium was built using the bricks from this building. (Courtesy of the Thomson–McDuffie County Library.)

The Thomson High School girls' basketball team of 1915 is seen here. Louise Dunn is seated in the first row on the far right. (Courtesy of William Dunn Wansley.)

Children pose on the steps of the Laura Jones School in Thomson. From left to right are (firs row) Louise Lasseter, Evelyn Gibson, Inez Harper, Alton Story, and Elizabeth Guye; (second row Hendree O'Neal, Marie Boyd, Bert Wilkerson, Neal Dunn, and ? Sills; (third row) unidentified, Stac Turner, Louise Smalley, Annie Sue Fanning, and unidentified; (fourth row) unidentified, Mildrec Farmer, Reese Guye, Pauline Maddox, and Claire Smith; (fifth row) unidentified, Irl Atkinson Robert Culbertson, Bertha Albert, and Agnes Reynolds. (Courtesy of Bunnie Hall Walden.)

This fifth grade class at Thomson High School included, from left to right, (first row) Boykir Wilson, Gene Dunn, Everette McCommons, Lillian Davey, ? Waters, and Gladys Morris; (seconc row) Harold Lokey, Lester Williams, Joel Dean, Durwood Smith, John F. Rivers, and J.E. Smith (third row) Virginia Bussey, Rad Story, John Morgan, unidentified, Marie Boyd, and Merle Story (fourth row) Virginia Price, Hubbard Samuels, unidentified, Sarah Shields, unidentified, and Johr Samuels; (fifth row) two unidentified, Gilbert Pilgrim, Eulon McCorkle, and two unidentified (sixth row) two unidentified and Thelma Mathews. (Courtesy of Bunnie Hall Walden.)

Students of Bertha Black's first-grade class at Dearing Elementary School are seen in April 1958. (Courtesy of Marcia Hardin Culpepper Harden.)

Dearing School seventh-graders pose for their class photograph. From left to right are (first row) Noel McGahee, Durham Clark, Donald Adair, Jack Aldred, Allen Mitchell, Peggy Gay, Betty Doris Neal, Juanita Holliman, Idelle Crosby, Ella Hardy, and Etta Ruth Anderson; (second row) John Gay, Clarence Newby, Julian Phillips, Durham Rabun, George Murphy, Margie Phillips, Louise Aycox, and Catherine Rabun; (third row) Dell Phillips, Ida B. Phillips, Betty Ivery, Elara Newby, and Mrs. Marion C. Connell. (Courtesy of Robin Wheelbarger Johnson.)

Graduating seniors from the Thomson High School class of 1928 pose with their diplomas. The stage curtain advertises R.A. Kunnes Department Store, Arnold Company, and J.M. Hayes (Courtesy of Suzanne Hunt Green.)

The Thomson High School football team is pictured with Coach Flash Gordon. Gen. Dewayne Patrick is the young boy at center wearing the No. 11 jersey. (Courtesy of John McBrayer.)

Pictured is Clio Perry's class on December 14, 1916, at Thomson Grammar School, later named Laura Jones Elementary School. From left to right are (first row) Marion Ancher, Ruby Smith, Gladys Farr, Rebekah Gary, Ruth Goolsby, and Jimmy Curtis; (second row) Mattie Sue Perry, Josie Smith, Nelson Dean, Julia Fanning, Helen Perry, and George Farmer. The rest are unidentified. (Courtesy of John McBrayer.)

This unidentified group of students are outside a school in Thomson in the early 1900s. (Courtesy of John McBrayer.)

Reeves Academy was one of the many one-room schoolhouses that graced McDuffie Count before schools were consolidated. The school was consolidated with Dearing by 1925. Dearin won a prize of $500 for being the first school in McDuffie County to consolidate three or mor schools and employ four or more teachers. (Courtesy of Sean Kelley.)

Students from the class of 1920 pose for their annual school photograph at Fort Creek School wit their teacher Anna Russell. Fort Creek School was just west of the Fort Creek Baptist Church The building was half on the church's property and half on property of Willie McGahee. Afte McDuffie County consolidated schools, the property was sold to Samuel McGahee for $40, wit Fort Creek Baptist Church receiving half of the sum. (Courtesy of Shirley Kelley Jones.)

Five

Places of the Past

A.L. McLean and J.T. Neal stand in front of an early bank in Thomson. (Courtesy of Rusty Lovelace.)

Employees of the Thomson Company outside the mill in May 1960. A large industry in Thomson, the Thomson Company manufactured clothes and was one of the largest employers in McDuffi

County for several decades. (Courtesy of Jimmy Crawley.)

This police booth once sat at the corner of Main and Railroad Streets in Thomson near the Thomson Depot. (Courtesy of Rusty Lovelace.)

This view looking west on Journal Street in Thomson shows the old Price Theatre and the building that housed the city hall and fire department. (Courtesy of Rusty Lovelace.)

Martha Ellen Cone Hunt sits with a child on their farm in the Wrightsboro community in the 1930s. (Courtesy of Suzanne Hunt Green.)

The Coca-Cola Bottling Company in Thomson was on Greenway Street. In 1948, it employed 12 people and operated four delivery trucks. The building now serves as the Thomson-McDuffie County Senior Center. (Courtesy of the McDuffie Museum.)

The Thomson Company clothing factory supported many middle-class families. The old company building is pictured here. (Courtesy of Rusty Lovelace.)

The McDuffie Oil and Fertilizer Company was founded in 1903 and was once a large employer. (Courtesy of Cindy Wilson.)

The old Rock Dam in the Wrightsboro community was constructed in 1771 by the Quaker settlers of the area. This historic landmark once diverted the waters of Maddock's Creek to a gristmill in the area. Epp Wilson is standing atop the old Rock Dam after its restoration. (Courtesy of Luckey Printing.)

The history of the Bowdre-Rees-Knox House goes back to the days of the Quaker village of Wrightsboro. Thomas Bowdre migrated to the area from Virginia in 1785 and married Ephatha Rees in 1805. The couple built the house near Wrightsboro around 1806. Bowdre later sold the home to Vincent Rees, a cousin of his wife. Rees's son E.B. Rees sold the house and 750 acres to T.A. Scott in February 1855. Peter Knox purchased the home and surrounding land in 1907. (Courtesy of Luckey Printing.)

The opening meet for the Belle Meade Hunt is held every year at the home pictured here, owned by Larry Knox. His father, Lawrence Knox, inherited the home and surrounding land from his father, P.S. Knox Sr. The house is built on the site of an earlier home known as the Hawes homeplace, pictured on page 99. The original home burned, and this house was built on the same foundation. (Courtesy of Sean Kelley.)

Sen. Tom Watson's death brought over 10,000 visitors to McDuffie County in 1922. Here, a large crowd is gathered outside of Watson's home, Hickory Hill. Senator Watson purchased the Wilson homeplace, including 121 acres, from J.E. Wilson, as well as "the John Neal lands," "the Texas place," and "the Brickyard place," on September 18, 1900. Watson renovated and made additions shortly after purchasing the home. (Courtesy of Rusty Lovelace.)

Pallbearers assist in laying Senator Watson to rest in the Thomson Memorial Cemetery on Tom Watson Way in Thomson. (Courtesy of Rusty Lovelace.)

James E. Harrison is standing alongside one of his horses for sale outside of his livery stable at the corner of Greenway and Journal Streets in the early 20th century. Prior to a fire that destroyed many buildings in downtown Thomson, Harrison's livery stable was on Main Street. (Courtesy of Edith Harrison Roth.)

Above, men stand inside Gibson's Drugstore. Below, men stand among the inventory in the old A&P store in downtown Thomson. Byrd Cloud "B.C." Perry is on the far right. (Above, courtesy of John McBrayer; below, courtesy of Rusty McGahee.)

This Hawes family photograph was taken around 1892 in front of their home in the Wrightsboro community. From left to right are Samuel Carlton Hawes, Ellington Charles Hawes, Samuel Carlton Hawes Jr., Amanda Wilson Hawes, Dr. Ellington Cody Hawes, John Ellis Hawes (with dog), and William Mosley Hawes held by an unidentified woman. Dr. Hawes was a state representative and one of the five men who pushed to establish McDuffie County. His grandson Ellington Charles Hawes was a state senator and president of the Bank of Thomson. John Ellis Hawes was a tax collector for McDuffie County. (Courtesy of John McBrayer.)

The Hunt homeplace, pictured in 1944, was purchased by Thomas H. Hunt and was located near Wrightsboro Church in the Wrightsboro community. (Courtesy of Suzanne Hunt Green.)

The Shields Country Store was across the road from the Shields homeplace and in front of Shield's Pond. (Courtesy of the Shields family.)

People are swimming, wading, and socializing at Shield's Pond in 1944. A portion of the bathhouse can be seen at top right. The popular swimming spot also offered swimming and safety classes. (Courtesy of the Shields family.)

This photograph shows the old mill building that once operated on Kiokee Creek and Shield's Pond. (Courtesy of the Shields family.)

William S. Shields Jr. is about to jump off the diving board into his family's pond. (Courtesy of the Shields family.)

Shield's Pond offered classes for those wishing to learn how to swim. This photograph was taken at Shield's Pond in 1952 and is likely of a group attending swimming lessons. Among those pictured are Jackie Mann and Doug Langford. (Courtesy of the Shields family.)

Louise Brown, far right, poses with children after a swimming class at Shield's Pond in 1952. (Courtesy of the Shields family.)

From left to right, Martha Harrison, Ned Harrison, and unidentified sit on horses in the front yard of the Harrison home on White Oak Street in Thomson in 1923. The home is still standing and looks the same. (Courtesy of Edith Harrison Roth.)

This is a glimpse of Main Street in downtown Thomson, the heart of McDuffie County, looking North. (Courtesy of Murray Boyd Beckum.)

People are gathered under the pavilion at Hunt's Lake in Boneville in 1910. (Courtesy of Rusty Lovelace.)

Men stand outside Thomson Filling Station on Jackson Street across from the Thomson Depot. At far right is Willie Lazenby. At a time when there was little funding for black children's education, Lazenby purchased the first school bus to transport African American students. On weekends, he also took adults places they wished to go, such as Augusta. (Courtesy of Rosa Lazenby Hunt.)

The Cotton Patch Motel was owned and operated by John Wilson. It was on Highway 78 near the original McDuffie County Hospital. Rooms were offered to Belle Meade Hunt riders at a reduced rate. (Courtesy of Rusty Lovelace.)

The Little River Bridge on the Thomson-Lincolnton Road is pictured here looking toward Thomson from Lincolnton on July 17, 1950, before Clarks Hill Lake flooded the area. The sign reads, "Bridge unsafe, travel at own risk." (Courtesy of Murray Boyd Beckum.)

The old McDuffie County jail sat on the corner of McDuffie Avenue and Church Street across from the historic McDuffie County Courthouse. The house served as part jail and part residence for the sheriff. Sheriff William Swan and his family resided here until it was torn down for the construction of the new jail. (Courtesy of the McDuffie Museum.)

The Knox-Neal Building served many purposes over the years. Here, signs on the building read "Post Office" and "Odd Fellows." It was also used for Dr. Neal's dentist office. The Rob L. Howell & Co. building at right housed the Idle Hour Café. The Howell building was also home to the Nehi bottling company. (Courtesy of Murray Boyd Beckum.)

The home of Rev. Aaron Adkins, known as "Brier Creek," was in the southwestern corner of the county. This was the home of the Gibson family for many years, but unfortunately, it is no longer standing. (Courtesy of William Dunn Wansley.)

People gather to witness the train that derailed in downtown Thomson near the Thomson Depot. The woman looking toward the camera with glasses is Pearl Kunnes, who operated the nearby Kunnes Department Store. (Courtesy of Murray Boyd Beckum.)

People stand on Main Street beside a Ford around 1931. In the background, the old Thomson Post Office, which now houses the Thomson-McDuffie Chamber of Commerce, is under construction (Courtesy of Murray Boyd Beckum.)

This early 1900s photograph shows a view of Main Street looking south. (Courtesy of Murray Boyd Beckum.)

Crawley's Hardware Store offered hardware supplies and contractor services. The old Coca-Cola sign above advertises minnows for sale, and window signs advertise Sherwin-Williams paints and roofing supplies. The new Crawley's building below, on West Hill Street, continued to sell building supplies as well as bicycles, paint, and the services of E.B. Baggett, jeweler. (Both, courtesy of City of Thomson.)

This photograph taken in the early 1950s shows the newly built McDuffie County Hospital on West Hill Street (Highway 278). (Courtesy of Sean Kelley.)

This postcard shows the old Thomson Post Office, built in 1931 on Main Street. The building is similar to the post office in Madison, Georgia. Both were constructed as part of the Works Progress Administration during the Great Depression. Note that the building once had windows along the mansard roof, which at some point were taken out and roofed over. (Courtesy of Bunnie Hall Walden.)

The Knox Hotel was built in 1850 by Joseph Henry Stockton and was originally named the Greenway Hotel. Charles Edward "Charlie" Knox purchased the hotel 32 years later, naming it the Knox Hotel. It was situated in the center of downtown Thomson and was a well-known landmark. (Courtesy of Murray Boyd Beckum.)

William A. "Top" Watson (left) and C.U. Hammett, claim agent of the Georgia Railroad, stand outside Watson's home on Church Street in Thomson about 1930. (Courtesy of Murray Boyd Beckum.)

The Dunn house, on Hall Street, was purchased from the Dunn family and torn down for the construction of a bank. (Courtesy of William Dunn Wansley.)

This photograph, taken in the 1940s, shows the front of the Alexandria Establishment. Alexandria, the oldest brick house in Georgia that can be documented to the date of construction, was built in 1803 by Thomas Carr. (Courtesy of William Dunn Wansley.)

This is the rear of the Alexandria Establishment in the 1950s. The back porch had been enclosed, and a fireplace was built for the original plantation office. These were later removed since they were not part of the original 1803 house. (Courtesy of William Dunn Wansley.)

In 2008, the Fort James chapter of the National Society Colonial Dames selected the Alexandria Establishment as a Colonial Dames designated historical site. Elizabeth Dunn Wansley is pictured beside a granite marker, which was placed on the Wansley property to commemorate the special event. (Courtesy of William Dunn Wansley.)

This c. 1920 photograph shows the Rousseau Springs Hotel and Spa in northern McDuffie County. The hotel was a popular destination in the 1920s and 1930s. The spring was said to have healing powers. (Courtesy of William Dunn Wansley.)

This was the home of Dr. William Martin in Cobbham, Georgia. It was listed on the original McDuffie County map of 1871. (Courtesy of William Dunn Wansley.)

This is one of the many houses that graced northern McDuffie County in the late 1800s. The house was located in Cobbham. (Courtesy of William Dunn Wansley.)

The JC Dunn Country Store was in Cobbham. (Courtesy of William Dunn Wansley.)

This home, which is still standing, is located on Cobbham Road and is currently owned by the Blount family. The home originally belonged to Thomas Watson, Sen. Tom Watson's grandfather. John Edward Smith purchased the home, known as "Ottley Hall," from John S. Watson (Thomas Watson's son) around 1867. The Smith family, a prominent family of McDuffie County, had a town home in Thomson where they lived during the school year and lived at Ottley Hall during the summer. (Courtesy of Bunnie Hall Walden.)

The Sara Smith Hall house is on Main Street beside the Thomson–McDuffie County Library. Sara Smith Hall inherited this house from her father, Baxter Smith. (Courtesy of Bunnie Hall Walden.)

The Knox-Walker-Beckum house is today Kay's Cut and Style, owned by Kay Kendrick. The house was built by Peter S. Knox Sr. around 1890 and is one of the oldest homes on Main Street in Thomson. Knox sold the home to Judge Benjamin Franklin Walker in 1898. The house's original appearance was altered by removing the steeple and adding a wraparound porch. Dora Ivey Walker is standing on the front steps around 1900. When the Walkers moved to another home in Thomson, this one was given to their daughter and son-in-law Orell Walker Beckum and William Forrest Beckum Sr. (Courtesy of Murray Boyd Beckum.)

The Boyd house was built around 1895 and did not have the elaborate porches and porticos. Mary Harriett Murray Boyd commissioned the construction of the porches, which took over a year to build. The house was later sold to Pete Knox and now serves as part of the Austin Oaks building. (Courtesy of Murray Boyd Beckum.)

The Goodrich House was erected in 1870 by two brothers from Connecticut. Timber used to build the house was cut from Briar Creek Swamp. It was constructed near the Printup Farm and the "Goody Railroad," which connected to the Georgia Railroad. Jim Linnenkohl purchased the home in 1940, and it has been in the Linnenkohl family since that time. (Courtesy of Ludwig Linnenkohl.)

The Smith-Hunt-Doughty house, more commonly known as the Dixie Inn, was built in 1881 and remodeled in 1920. The house was used as a hotel for those who traveled to Boneville. The Dixie Inn overlooked the Boneville Millpond, also known as Hunt's Lake or Camellia Lake, and was situated behind a rock wall. Unfortunately, the house burned in recent years. (Courtesy of the McDuffie County Historic Preservation Commission.)

The Lavigno Mercantile Company, built around 1910 in Boneville, was a small country store operated by Rock Lavigno. (Courtesy of the McDuffie County Historic Preservation Commission.)

The oldest house in Boneville is the Rock Lavigno House, which was built in 1873. The Lavigno family operated a store in Boneville, as well as a syrup mill, and grew various crops on their 100-acre farm. Rock Lavigno's daughter-in-law Willie Belle Lavigno operated the nearby Dixie Inn in the 1920s. (Courtesy of the McDuffie County Historic Preservation Commission.)

The Boneville Mill, built in 1845, was used to manufacture cards used for carding cotton. Ownership transferred in 1872, and the new owners began manufacturing flour, meal, and shoes. In 1877, the mill was sold again and became a sawmill and gristmill. A flood in 1941 damaged the mill, and it was never repaired or reopened. The mill was powered from the waters of Boneville Millpond, which was later renamed Camellia Lake by Clyde Forrest "C.F." Hunt. Camellia Lake was a popular recreational spot. (Courtesy of the McDuffie County Historic Preservation Commission.)

Arrington's Mill is on Fort Creek Road, previously called Arrington's Mill Road. Around 1840 Howard Hobbs built the mill and dam to run a sawmill. At some point, the property was transferred from Howard Hobbs to Samuel Megahee. Around 1913–1915, George W. Arrington and Ruby Hobbs Arrington purchased the mill from Mary Ann Megahee, widow of Samuel Megahee. (Courtesy of Debbie Arrington Gunn.)

The Printup house, outside of Dearing, was built in 1863 by William Printup. After the death of William Printup in 1893, his eldest son, John Robert Printup, purchased the home and farm. The house was passed to Robert Earl Printup when his father died in 1920. (Courtesy of Teresa Printup Putnam.)

The Cassell house in Dearing was owned by Jenny Clark. "Miss Jenny," standing third from left, is pictured with a group of women and children. When the school in Dearing burned on February 3, 1937, temporary classrooms were set up in this house, as well as in the barbershop, old bank building, and other vacant buildings in town. (Courtesy of Laura Parker.)

Whitaker Dairy Farm began in the early 1950s on L.B. Whitaker's farm about five miles southeas of Dearing. His son Theron "Bo" Whitaker managed the farm during his lifetime. The barn seen here is the original dairy barn, with cattle numbering around 100. In 1962, a modern barn wa built. (Courtesy of Sean Kelley.)

Lloyd and Lucille Rodgers moved their family to a farm they purchased from J. Gordon Usry in 1942. The farm, on Iron Hill Road, started out with two milk cows, which Lucille used to sell milk. Through hard work and dedication, the Rodgers family built a family dairy business from two cows in 1941 to 820 in 2020. The farm is now in the capable hands of sons Andy and Mark Rodgers and grandchildren Caitlyn and Joshua. (Courtesy of the Rodgers family.)

Joe's Service Station was on Augusta Highway in Dearing. In 1961 gas is advertised at 25.9¢ and 27.9¢ a gallon. Miss Allene's Sandwich Shop is in the background across the road. (Courtesy of Sean Kelley.)

Sammie Kelley is sitting on the front porch of the old Dearing Pool Room at the corner of South Main and Reeves Streets. Kelley operated the pool hall, which also sold snacks, in the late 1960s. He sold peanuts for 10¢ a bag and three large pieces of peanut brittle, prepared by his mother, Mary Katherine Kelley, for 20¢. (Courtesy of Sean Kelley.)

Here is Charlie Taylor's store on Augusta Highway in Dearing in the 1950s. The store was located where Axon's Mini Mart is today. (Courtesy of Sean Kelley.)

Pictured are Loyd Welch (1893–1961) and his mother, Jennie Welch (1869–1954), on the front porch of their home on Mattie Harrison Road. The Welch family lived on Walker Road in a house that was converted from an old schoolhouse. The old Fairview School building is still standing on Walker Road. An article in the *Augusta Chronicle* in 1958 recognized Loyd Welch as the only blind subscriber to the newspaper. Welch's disability did not keep him from working hard to provide for his family. Not only did he run a store out of their home that sold canned goods and other necessities, he also operated a grist mill on the property. (Courtesy of Daisy Pearl Welch McCorkle.)

Ray Adams is standing in front of his service station and grocery store that he operated from the 1940s until 1953, when he built Dearing Supermarket on an adjacent lot. The left wing of the building included an auto mechanic shop. (Courtesy of Richard Adams.)

Cars line the street in this photograph of Railroad Street looking west from the intersection of Greenway Street. Buildings advertise Mack's Mercantile and Hoyt Gunby's groceries. The Thomson–McDuffie County Government Center is now across from this intersection. (Courtesy of Rusty Lovelace.)

The Thomson–McDuffie County Government Center was built in 2011 to house the courts and government administrative offices in one building. On the 150th anniversary of McDuffie County, this building will serve as the heart of the commemorative festival honoring the heritage of McDuffie County. (Courtesy of McDuffie County.)

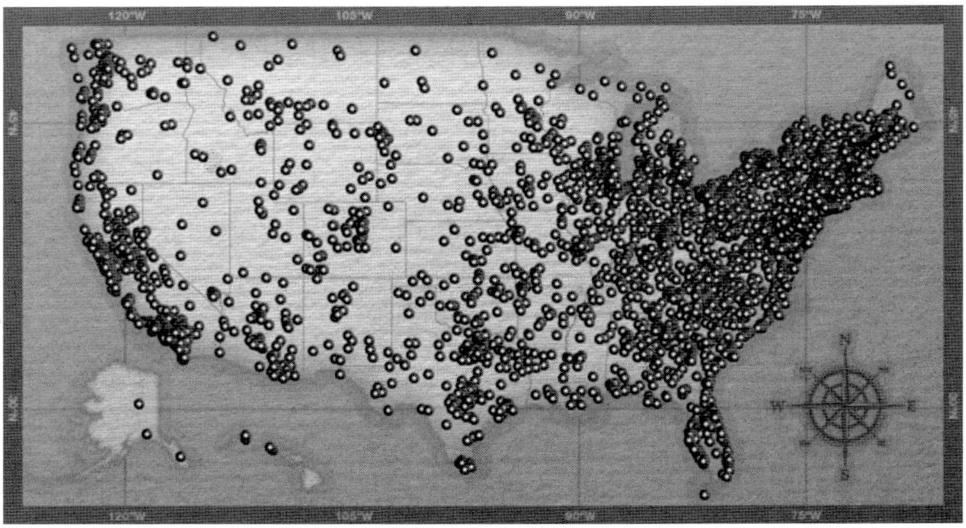

Consistent with our mission to preserve history on a local level, this book was printed in South Carolina on American-made paper and manufactured entirely in the United States. Products carrying the accredited Forest Stewardship Council (FSC) label are printed on 100 percent FSC-certified paper.

MADE IN THE USA